On the Other Side of Fear

Julia Fehrenbacher

Copyright © 2012 Julia Fehrenbacher.

All rights reserved. No part of this book may be used or reproduced by any means, graphic, electronic, or mechanical, including photocopying, recording, taping or by any information storage retrieval system without the written permission of the publisher except in the case of brief quotations embodied in critical articles and reviews.

Balboa Press books may be ordered through booksellers or by contacting:

Balboa Press
A Division of Hay House
1663 Liberty Drive
Bloomington, IN 47403
www.balboapress.com
1-(877) 407-4847

Because of the dynamic nature of the Internet, any web addresses or links contained in this book may have changed since publication and may no longer be valid. The views expressed in this work are solely those of the author and do not necessarily reflect the views of the publisher, and the publisher hereby disclaims any responsibility for them.

ISBN: 978-1-4525-5104-3 (sc)
ISBN: 978-1-4525-5103-6 (e)

Any people depicted in stock imagery provided by Thinkstock are models, and such images are being used for illustrative purposes only.
Certain stock imagery © Thinkstock.

Printed in the United States of America

Balboa Press rev. date: 5/30/2012

BALBOA PRESS
A DIVISION OF HAY HOUSE

To you who ache and want and doubt and sometimes forget—who, despite so much, find the courage to return, again and again, to love.

To you who held my hand along the way, who wholeheartedly saw and believed in this book before I did. Thank you for helping me to see and believe.

To my little girls, Marielle and Lily, and my husband, Matt, who continually remind me of what matters most.

To you, wise, unconditional one within, who so gently and faithfully holds and loves no matter what.

Contents

A Note From Julia ix
Dear You 1
Complete 3
No Matter What 4
Wide-Eyed Open 7
Release 9
Emptying 11
Unleashed 12
Us 15
The Poetry of it All 17
Remembering 18
Now 21
Can You? 22
Like the Moon 24
It 25
What They're Saying 27
Follow Me 29
Freefall 30
Unconditional 31
Finding the Words 33
The Light 34
Held 36
Living Piece of Art 37
I Am 39
Do You Dare? 40
Listening 43
On the Other Side of Fear 45
For This You Came 47
You 48

A Note From Julia

One thing I know with absolute certainty is that when I drop below the level of thought and step fully into the moment I'm in, my insides soften, my breath deepens, a quiet, yet powerful knowing meets me right where I am. *On the Other Side of Fear* is about accessing this sacred space, the space that isn't concerned with rightdoing or wrongdoing, changing or fixing—it is about turning toward the space where softness rests and hunger fades.

I have learned through many years of unlearning and looking closely, that when I make a conscious choice to move forward, even when my voice shakes (like now, for example), even when the safety net is nowhere in sight, magic happens. Freedom happens. A world of possibility that my mind can't possibly fathom opens wide before me.

When I sit down to write poetry or pause before a blank canvas, it is my intention to get out of the way and allow something fresh and rich to flow through me, something beyond the confines of my limited mind. Each time I sit down, the process begins again. It seems it's always the same. My mind jumps in with its gripping resistance and informs me of all the reasons I'm not good enough, insisting that I don't have what it takes, that I should or shouldn't do it this or that way. Each time, moment by moment, I must quiet the noise of my mind, tune in and simply (and not so simply) allow and trust that this sacred presence knows just what to do/write/paint. I breathe deep breaths, sometimes I pray or sip hot tea or light a candle or all of the above. Sometimes I flail around for hours or days or weeks before that noisiness decides to fade to something like quiet. Or until I move despite (or maybe because of) the noise.

Regardless, my intention, my practice, is to keep returning to what is right before me, to pause long enough to allow my heart to take the lead, to find beauty even when it appears there is none.

It is clear to me that, as humans, we are always in the midst of creation. Just as we write one word at a time or paint one brush stroke at a time, life unfolds one breath at a time. In each new moment we can make a conscious choice to let go and allow something new to flow through us. In each new moment we are challenged to come back, to quiet our minds, to let go of what no longer serves us, so that we may meet what is right before us directly and wholeheartedly, so that we may live life on the other side of fear rather than allowing it to take hold and stop us in our tracks.

My greatest desire, and my greatest challenge, is to live wide awake, to live with courage and aliveness, to meet what is with the fullness of me and to nudge others toward the same. This book is my answer to that desire, my wholehearted offering from me to me, from me to you.

I invite you to join me on this wild, bumpy, heart-opening ride of waking up to the You that is not limited by narrow definitions or constricting judgments, to waking up to life just as it is.

May the words and paintings on these pages be like a hand that takes yours and nudges you gently inward. May the creations that have begun to free my wings help to free yours. Here's to doing a little moving, a little shimmying, maybe even a little flying together.

I am so very happy you are here with me.

With so much love,

Julia

*Take my hand, let's roam
let's pause
at the edge of the stream*

*no wants
no words
no worries*

*just the Light in you dancing
with the Light
that is me*

Dear You

You, the one reading these words
you, with your ancient, wanting heart
you, wondering if you'll ever
get it right

I invite you to pause
for a moment
to listen to the space
between
these words
to the space where softness
rests
and hunger
fades

to the space that so
gently
asks you to
stop
the thoughts
that doubt your worth
to stop the voices that compare
and leave you feeling
less

There is no less
there are no shadows or shoulds, no pretty or good
no bad or broken, no right or wrong in
Love

There is only this breath
and that which breathes it
there is only You
and your giggling, fully blossomed
Self

ready
ready right now
to shine
its newborn
ancient
just right
Light

Whispers of Truth

Complete

If only we could be as brave
as that tall growing oak
rooted deeply to the warm earth
It reaches its naked branches
up to the sun
and drops its leaves
one by one
never once stopping
to cling or hold on
or question
or long

Just a tree
being a tree
being a tree

No Matter What

I see

you are just like me
achingly wanting
achingly waiting
achingly yearning
to sprout, to bud, to blossom
into the whole, sacred essence
of you

I see little girl you
who lost and never found
who wanted but never got
who saw but was seldom
Seen

I see ancient woman you
how deeply
she wants to be loved
for her shadows as much as her light
how deeply
she wants to be embraced
for her wild
and her tender

I see
I am here
to remind you
that you no longer
need to shrink in order to fit in
you no longer need to contain
what isn't containable
you no longer need to be
the convenient version of what you think
they want you to be

I see
I am here to invite you
to lean the tenderness of you
into the tenderness of me

to promise
not to try to solve
or fix
or wish anything away

to promise
to love you
no matter what

Let Go and Let Love

Wide-Eyed Open

I would have missed this

You, baby bird
with your half- broken wing
you, with your tiny freckles
and eyes that plead
please, please love me
just the way I am

I would have missed this
if I had held back the gush
of love
in that one-of-a-kind moment
the one that will never
be again

wispy angel clouds
hand reaching for mine
breath full of new
I would have missed you

if I'd been bound
by what was appropriate
by whether they'd approve
by should or shouldn't haves
what ifs or hows
if I had been measuring
or grasping, wishing
I had
or hadn't
If I had been thinking
this moment needed
to be more
or less

I would have missed this
but I didn't, thank God
instead I was right

Here

wide-eyed open
heartfirst diving
into this sparkling
never ending
sea of
You

Release

This morning
as my eyes blink
open
it occurs to me
as if for the first time
what you, miracle body, have been up to

All night long, while I let go
you pumped blood through veins
to fingertips and toes
grew cells and eyelashes and nails
inhaled and exhaled
countless times

all this while the sun
tirelessly
birthed new
life

all this without a thought or a word
or a worry
without a drop of help
from me

I laugh when I remember
that just yesterday in a torrent
of heart-numbing
stories

i seriously thought
i
needed to do something

Just right

Just Right

Emptying

Tangled
in old stories
I circle around
and around, forgetting all
I know

I try
to stand still
to fix the broken parts
to be
the one who is okay

I wish I hadn't
I should have
if only
I had accepted
instead of pushed away

I hold too many pictures
of the wrong things
the ugliness
of too many lifetimes
trapped inside

I don't want to be the keeper anymore.

I will
empty myself
again and again
and again

until all that is left is
Quiet
and a Knowing
that it is all
right

Just as it was
Just as it is

Unleashed

What is this?

This thirst
this hunger
this feeling that tugs
and pulses and
saturates
every blink

every breath

This feeling of wanting
to stand at the highest
of high places—
limbs stretched out, like branches
or wings

and bow
with the whole
of my weeping
laughing
YES-ing
Voice

to my singing
feathered friends
to roots and buds and blossoms
to puddles and oceans and
awakened little streams
to the lily
that almost blooms
but not quite
to the just-born lamb
that hasn't yet
found the ground

And to you, dear heart—
with all of your bruises
and scars and open wounds
with all of your courage

and hesitation and astonishing
Beauty

I want to pour
out my
YES-es
as if
Life
depends on it

because
I'm really quite certain
It
does

Sharing a Moment

Us

Remember the beginning
how we sat crossed-legged
knees brushing knees
while you fed me mango
one slow bite
after another

eyes seeing
all the way
inside
to the deepest parts

We kissed
in produce aisles,
next to blooming Rhododendrons
in wide open meadows
where wild flowers grew

Between juicy bites
and slow sips of red wine
you told me.
Not with words
but with hands
and eyes

and layer after
layer fell
away
leaving behind
a fullness
calm and cloudless
and sure

Then came the *I dos,* morning sickness,
middle-of-the-night feedings
toddlers and tantrums
interruptions
and disagreements
over who should
or shouldn't, who did
or didn't

And the insatiable need for sleep.

But under layers
of heavy storm clouds
that clear sky
remains

Still and sure
and waiting
for our quiet
Return

The Poetry of it All

The way the Light kisses
the snowberry as if for the last time
the way the dew drop holds on for dear life
before it lets go
the way
the two winged ones share
the same fragile branch

makes me want to live better

Makes me want to, for all the rest of my days
bow and weep and sing
Hallelujah!
and promise to stay forever
wide-eyed Awake
to the undeniable poetry
of it all

Remembering

There is nothing you need to do, you know

no amount of hiding or seeking
or telling or trying will erase
the ache, the weight
the trembling, strangling
middle of the moment
grip
that threatens to feast
on your core

You need only
return
to the part
that breathes
and beats and hears
and Sees
all on its very own

to the part that hums
and sways and dreams
lullabies

of Peace

Come, it says
lean the weight of you
against me
sit and stay

until you remember

that you are tangled
and woven
in stardust
in roots and rivers
in suns and moons
in every breath
that has ever breathed

until you remember

that you are Me
and I am You
that together we
Are

everything

Breathe Peace

Now

Without words
we sit in quiet.
Stillness wraps
around us
in its soft, electric way

There is no wanting
or needing to know
what comes next
no questions
or place to get
we are not
tangled
in yesterdays
or turning toward
tomorrow

Just us
and something
that will
remain
through births
and deaths
and lifetimes

infinite nows from now
infinite nows from then

Can You?

Can you, for just a minute
leave
the white tablecloth, the washing
the sorting, the scanning
the lists, the date books
the .coms, the inbox
the goals, the resolutions
the plans, the labels, the schedule, the old
stories
the scars, the scales, the bruises
the pains, the aches
the what ifs, the should haves
the pointing fingers
the too small boxes
the questions, the containers
the dividers, the protectors
the sickening
paralyzing
expectations?

Can you, for just a minute
hush
the voices that howl madly
at your old, tired
little self?

For a brave minute or two
can you pry open the bars

and listen
to the wordless—
to the hum
between
to that which births snowflakes
and stars and sighs
and moonlit little streams?

On this frozen winter night
when your heart
especially needs warming, I'm wondering

can you, for just a minute
get quiet enough to hear
the silent
flutter
of this one precious
life
of this one
precious breath?

Like the Moon

You are here in this world
to Love
to lay down the swords—the armor
to fall down laughing, to swing
amongst the stars

to lean into everything
that makes your heart flutter
to live with unapologetic brightness

like the moon

It

I've been looking
for It
all day

in rain-soaked sidewalks
in the lit tip of his cigarette
in the threads
of the canvas, in the ink
dripping
off this page

studying
naked branches
and dew drops about to fall. Praying
that I'll find It
there
in things I can see
and name

as if It
can be reeled in
and caught

as if
It
can be found
in things out
there

Breathe

What They're Saying

The birds, the shadows
the leaves
every granule
of sand, they're all saying
the same thing

Slow way down
get close and closer
listen like crazy
to your life

Create with Abandon

Follow Me

She refuses
to listen anymore
to tiny can't-ing voices
that force the lid
on what
Never
should have been
boxed

She refuses
to limit
any of it anymore
with recycled thoughts
of shoulds
and shouldn'ts

Silly little mind
you no longer get to
decide

Her insides are bursting, beaming
Screaming
I'm ready!

Love says
follow me

every ray in her
whispers

Fly Now
You are Free

Freefall

Fall back
fall all the way back
let the current
carry you

open wide
to the smiling sun
to the laughing moon, to clouds
and trees and bees and butterflies

They all know
as the river knows
as the twinkling little stars know

as your open, big heart knows
when the rest gets out of the way

Fall back
dance with the storm clouds
let *all the way go*
and be carried
the whole way
the whole way back

to your open
laughing
Home

Unconditional

I want to crawl inside
your heart space
curl up tight and close
and silently allow
it to massage me
with its many notes
and rhythms
I want to stay
there for a moment or maybe
an eternity
feeling every bit of everything
you feel. I don't
want to miss a beat
or run
when it gets to be
too much
I want to stay and stay.
With each rhythmic pulse
with every pang
and blossom; I want
to stay

You are so Loved

Finding the Words

Where are the words, she asked
and why don't they come out all sparkly clear
and clean, like hers
or his
why must i work so hard to shine
my shine
when all I want is to

Be
like the ancient oak
to open
my wings
like those cormorants do

Why, rather than sailing with
the current
must i turn my back on it
when all I want, all I've forever wanted
is to empty the fullness of me
like the sky empties rain

a torrential downpour

that leaves us quenched
and drenched
blissfully basking in
the mind-blowing glory
of You

The Light

In this patch of sunlight
she writes
and wants
and waits
for something that will not come.
Steam rises
from the cold, wet grass
a single droplet
lets go
of the oak leaf.

It does not matter
what happened yesterday
or even a moment ago
the trees do not remember.
They do not
wait either, as she
does now.
They know
this full moment
is all
there is
that within it
rests
the Sun.

Feeling the Ground

Held

When she slows
quietly down
instead of pushing
urgently forward
When she asks and listens
and receives
instead of talking and telling
and trying
When she bows
deeply
to this light-filled
Now
instead of running
screaming away
It bows deeply back

and she feels herself
falling

freely
falling
safely
falling
softly
falling
back into
the wide open
arms
of Grace

Living Piece of Art

For a moment today
I forgot
all that "needed" improving.

The growing pile of laundry
the nagging to do list

I forgot to care
whether I was on the right path
which direction I should go
or how I would get there

I simply pressed pause
and watched your tiny sunlit hands
pluck one dandelion
after another
until you had a perfect
sweet bouquet

then you skipped down the hill
while the angels sang
and my heart followed you
home

Beginnings

I Am

It's not that I don't want to feel
the wind
of a thousand wild storms
or dance in the blaze
of one electrifying kiss

It's just that, in the midst
of it all
I want to be
clear
like crystal is clear
calm
like that old sleepy oak

So deep down rooted
and wide-armed welcoming
of what
IS

that even when the ground trembles
and crumbles
beneath me

I See
like the mountain Sees

I Am

the life-giving
Breath
at the center
of it all

Do You Dare?

Are you willing, in the name of Truth

to be unliked, unloved
misunderstood
to feel shaky-voiced afraid
"not ready"
and to say yes! anyway?

Are you willing to stretch
in the direction of the moon
even when those old voices
say their old things
do you dare stretch anyway
show up anyway
do it anyway?

Are you willing
to sob when you feel like sobbing
laugh when it's not "appropriate"
raise your voice
when it's "better" to be quiet?

Are you willing to turn the faucet all the way on
even while you're being cautioned
to be careful
to be safe, to be realistic?

Are you willing to stay awake
no matter how sleepy you are
no matter what's happening or isn't
no matter what they say
or don't say?

Are you willing to Trust
even when the only step you see is
this one
to be directionless, without a map
a path, a past
or a plan?

Are you willing to fall back
all the way back
to release your grip
on all you thought
you knew
break free
from your boxes
tear down the walls
trust that love
is your best protection, the only thing
that's Real?

Are you willing to embrace
your quirks and "flaws"
find the gifts In your "mistakes"
and theres
to shine your shine
no matter what
to Love no matter what
to Trust
no matter what?

Are you willing to wait
when it's not yet time
to leap when it is
to shed, unravel, peel away, let go
until you are left with only
Real?

Are you willing to lean toward, lean into
that which cannot be bound
to brush the moon with your fingertips
to go beyond
what is beyond
to let go of trying to be "good" if it means
stepping toward Love
toward whatever
makes you gasp
and grin and giggle?

Tell me, are you willing? Do you dare?

Coming Home

Listening

What if I just sit here
right now
and maybe
forever

sipping tea
and poetry, breathing in
each word
like it's all
that will keep me
alive

Listening

as the right now
wild rain
grows wilder

just the two of us
side by side
pouring
our thirsty hearts
all over the place

Fearless Me

On the Other Side of Fear

You don't have to wait

a second longer
to move
to step
to shimmy
through that mirage
of can'ts and not
enough-ness

You don't have to *try*
to be
something you've always been
something you can't
not be.

Breather of life
one who cannot be contained
or named
one who sleeps and dreams
and wakes
who forgets and stumbles
who hungers
to be Seen
and understood

one who despite—
despite so much
returns
and returns
to Love

I know how very tired you are.

You can let go now.
You can let go of those mountains
you carry.
You don't have to wait
a breath longer to be
all you ache
to be

all you so perfectly are.

Simply breathe
a breath so wide—
so cracked-open wide
even the moon
enters. And the two of you
with your galaxy full
of Light
with your naked wide-
openness

can shimmy
can shimmy right through
to the other side

For This You Came

Roll down the windows
throw open the doors
dip your toes in magenta
burnt umber, cobalt blue

Let yourself sing off-key

For this you came
to show up
Here
to swim and splash
in the shimmering palette
of you

to make something out of nothing.

What good is "good" or "safe"
when you can have spilling over laughter
heart-melting connection
breath-giving moments
of Real?

Rip off your life preservers
stop clinging to the shore
of what makes sense

Turn the sky upside down

Let faith be your shelter
your candle, your torch
your one and only
safety net

With hand over heart
in this right now moment
say yes!
a leaping-with-the-whole-of-your-body
YES

to your Life

You

I love you

because you're here
because our feet kiss the same ground
because when you find your roar
your roar finds me

I love you
because you ache and giggle
because you don't always get it "right"
because when it pours
we both get drenched

I love you with my whole wide singing heart
because in your eyes I See
all
you think you're not

I love you
because I meet myself
in the furrow of your brow
because in the curve of your smile
I smile too

Take my hand, let's roam
let's pause
at the edge of the stream
no wants
no words
no worries
just the Light in you dancing
with the Light
that is me

Printed in Great Britain
by Amazon